Carter Godwin Woodson

The Biography, Career, and Legacy of the Father of Black History, Including the Inside Story of His Struggles for Racial Justice.

Ben Richardson

Carter Godwin Woodson

Copyright © Ben Richardson 2024

Dedicated to Carter G. Woodson—his vision, dedication, and legacy illuminate the path to understanding and equality.

Table Of Content

Introduction

In the history of the United States, few individuals have left as profound a mark as Carter G. Woodson. Born into poverty in New Canton, Virginia, in 1875, Woodson's journey from the coal mines of West Virginia to becoming the pioneer of African American history is a testament to resilience and determination. His life's work centered on the recognition and celebration of the contributions of Black Americans to the tapestry of American history.

Woodson's significance lies not only in his own accomplishments but also in his unwavering commitment to ensuring that the stories of African Americans were not relegated to the sidelines of history. At a time when the achievements of Black people were largely ignored or misrepresented in mainstream education and scholarship, Woodson took it upon himself to fill this gap.

Through his groundbreaking research, writing, and advocacy, Woodson laid the foundation for the academic study of African American history. His efforts led to the establishment of the Association for the Study of Negro Life and History (now the Association for the Study of African American Life and History) in 1915, providing a platform for scholars to explore and disseminate knowledge about Black history.

One of Woodson's most enduring legacies is the creation of Negro History Week in 1926, which later evolved into Black History Month. By designating a specific time to focus on the achievements and struggles of African Americans, Woodson aimed to challenge prevailing notions of racial inferiority and highlight the integral role of Black people in shaping the nation's history.

As we delve into the life and legacy of Carter G. Woodson, we uncover not only the remarkable accomplishments of a pioneering historian but also the enduring impact of his work on our understanding of American history. His story serves as a reminder of the importance of recognizing and honoring the contributions of all individuals, regardless of race or background, to the rich tapestry of human experience.

Chapter One

Early Life and Education

Carter Godwin Woodson's life begins on December 19, 1875, in New Canton, Virginia. He was born into a family of former slaves, Anne Eliza and James Henry Woodson. Despite their own struggles, Woodson's parents instilled in him a deep appreciation for education and a strong sense of pride in their African American heritage.

Growing up in poverty, Woodson faced numerous challenges, including limited access to formal education. However, his parents recognized the importance of learning and encouraged him to pursue knowledge through self-instruction. Despite having to help out on the family farm, Woodson managed to educate himself with the help of his mother and uncles, who were also taught to read.

At the age of seventeen, Woodson moved to Huntington, West Virginia, with the hope of attending Douglass High School, a secondary school for African Americans. However, financial constraints forced him to work in the coal mines near New River, leaving little time for his studies. Despite these obstacles, Woodson's determination remained steadfast.

It wasn't until he turned twenty that Woodson was able to enroll full-time at Douglass High School. He finally received his diploma in 1897, marking a significant achievement in his pursuit of education. Following his graduation, Woodson worked as a teacher at a school in Winona, West Virginia, where he continued to inspire young minds.

Woodson's thirst for knowledge led him to pursue further education at Berea College in Kentucky, where he earned his bachelor's degree in literature in 1903. He then embarked on a journey to the Philippines, serving as a school supervisor from 1903 to 1907. Despite facing racial discrimination and adversity, Woodson remained committed to his academic pursuits.

Chapter Two

Higher Education and Early Career

After obtaining his high school diploma and teaching experience, Carter G. Woodson's journey continued with his enrollment at Berea College in Kentucky. Here, he delved into the realm of higher education, eager to expand his understanding of literature.

Woodson's time at Berea College marked a significant chapter in his academic pursuits, providing him with a foundation for the intellectual feats that would follow.

In 1903, Woodson proudly earned his bachelor's degree in literature. This achievement not only reflected his dedication to education but also set the stage for his future endeavors. With a degree in hand, Woodson's passion for learning led him to new horizons, taking him far beyond the borders of the United States.

From 1903 to 1907, Woodson served as a school supervisor in the Philippines. This period abroad not only broadened his cultural experiences but also presented him with the challenges and triumphs of education on an international scale.

Woodson's commitment to improving educational systems and fostering knowledge persisted, even in the face of the complexities of working in a foreign land.

Upon his return to the United States, Woodson continued his academic journey with a focus on advanced degrees. The University of Chicago became the next stop on his path to intellectual growth. Woodson's dedication and scholarly pursuits resulted in the award of both an A.B. (Bachelor of Arts) and an A.M. (Master of Arts) in 1908.

His time at the University of Chicago solidified his place among the academic elite and laid the groundwork for his future contributions to African American history.

Woodson's commitment to education extended beyond the classroom. His membership in Sigma Pi Phi, the first Black professional fraternity, and Omega Psi Phi, a fraternity founded on principles of scholarship and service, reflected his dedication to fostering academic excellence and community upliftment.

The pinnacle of Woodson's academic journey came in 1912 when he completed his Ph.D. in history at Harvard University. Notably, he became the second African American to earn a doctorate from Harvard, following in the footsteps of the esteemed W. E. B. Du Bois.

Chapter Three

Professional Roles

Carter G. Woodson's professional journey was not without its challenges, particularly in securing a university position. Despite his impressive academic achievements, Woodson faced discrimination and reluctance from universities to hire him.

Undeterred by these obstacles, he embarked on a mission to carve out a space for Black historians within the academic landscape, recognizing the need for an inclusive and representative historical narrative.

Woodson's career advanced in 1900 when he assumed the role of principal at Armstrong Manual Training School. This marked a significant milestone, as it was the same institution where he had initially started his academic career. His tenure as principal showcased his leadership abilities and commitment to educational excellence.

Subsequently, Woodson's professional journey led him to Howard University, a historically Black institution. Joining the faculty at Howard was a pivotal move that allowed him to contribute to the academic development of Black students and further solidify his standing within the African American intellectual community.

Woodson's impact at Howard University continued to grow, leading to his appointment as Dean of the College of Arts and Sciences. In this role, he played a crucial part in shaping the educational experiences of countless students, fostering an environment that valued the contributions of Black scholars to various disciplines.

His perception of the American Historical Association (AHA) became increasingly critical. Woodson noted the AHA's lack of interest in Black history, exemplified by his exclusion from AHA conferences despite being a dues-paying member. This realization fueled Woodson's conviction that the white-dominated historical profession was not conducive to the recognition of Black history within mainstream academia.

Undeterred by the systemic barriers, Woodson recognized the need to establish an institutional structure that would support Black historians. He understood that creating opportunities for Black scholars to study and contribute to history required financial backing and support. To achieve this vision, Woodson sought the assistance of philanthropic institutions such as the Carnegie Foundation, the Julius Rosenwald Foundation, and the Rockefeller Foundation.

Woodson's endeavors were not just about his personal advancement; they were rooted in a broader mission to ensure the representation and recognition of Black history within the academic sphere. His efforts laid the foundation for the establishment of the Association for the Study of Negro Life and History in 1915, signaling a turning point in the systematic inclusion of Black voices in historical discourse.

Chapter Four

Founding the ASNLH

In 1915, Carter G. Woodson, along with like-minded scholars including William D. Hartgrove, George Cleveland Hall, Alexander L. Jackson, and James E. Stamps, founded the Association for the Study of Negro Life and History (ASNLH). This pivotal moment marked the beginning of a concerted effort to rectify the neglect and misrepresentation of African American history within academic circles.

The mission and objectives of ASNLH were clear and resolute. Woodson aimed to systematically study and publish findings related to the neglected aspects of Negro life and history. The Association sought to contribute scientifically to the understanding of the African American experience and, in doing so, counter the prevailing notion that Black history was negligible in the broader scope of world history.

At the heart of ASNLH's initiatives was the Journal of Negro History, initiated by Woodson in January 1916. This scholarly publication became a cornerstone of the Association's endeavors, consistently publishing research that delved into various aspects of African American history.

Despite facing challenges such as the Great Depression, loss of support from foundations, and the upheavals of two

World Wars, the Journal of Negro History endured. In 2002, it was renamed the Journal of African American History and continued to be published by the Association for the Study of African American Life and History (ASALH).

ASNLH didn't limit itself to academic publications. The Association actively organized conferences that brought together scholars, educators, and researchers to discuss and share insights into African American history. These conferences provided a platform for intellectual exchange and laid the groundwork for collaborative efforts to advance the understanding of Black history.

Woodson envisioned ASNLH as a catalyst for educating Black civic leaders and teachers. He believed that through education and increased social and professional contacts between Black and white individuals, racism could be reduced.

ASNLH, under Woodson's leadership, sought to engage a broad audience, including high school teachers, clergymen, women's groups, and fraternal associations. The ultimate goal was to dispel misconceptions, challenge biases, and foster a comprehensive understanding of African American contributions to history.

Chapter Five

Negro History Week and

Black History Month

In 1926, Carter G. Woodson pioneered the concept of Negro History Week, marking a significant milestone in the recognition and celebration of African American history. Woodson chose the second week in February for this observance to coincide with the birthdays of two influential figures in African American history: Abraham Lincoln and Frederick Douglass.

By aligning Negro History Week with these notable dates, Woodson aimed to underscore the intertwined legacies of emancipation and abolitionism in the African American experience.

Over time, Negro History Week evolved into Black History Month, expanding its scope and duration to encompass the entire month of February. This transition reflected a growing recognition of the need for a more extensive and sustained focus on African American history and achievements.

Black History Month provided a platform for communities to engage in meaningful discussions, educational activities, and cultural celebrations that highlighted the contributions of African Americans to society.

Public engagement and celebrations during Black History Month have been diverse and widespread, encompassing various forms of expression such as parades, lectures, art exhibitions, film screenings, and musical performances. These events serve not only to educate and inform but also to inspire and empower individuals of all backgrounds to appreciate the richness and diversity of African American heritage.

At the core of Negro History Week and later Black History Month is the objective of emphasizing the Negro in history. Woodson recognized the need to rectify the historical omissions and misrepresentations that had marginalized African American contributions to the narrative of human progress.

By dedicating specific time and attention to the study and celebration of Black history, Woodson sought to ensure that the voices and experiences of African Americans were acknowledged, respected, and integrated into the broader tapestry of world history.

Chapter Six

Criticisms and Controversies

Woodson's positive view of Black history faced criticisms, particularly from those who argued that his approach may have been overly optimistic or idealized. Some critics contended that Woodson's emphasis on highlighting the achievements and contributions of African Americans might lead to a skewed portrayal, overlooking challenges and complexities inherent in the historical experiences of Black communities.

Debates surrounding the representation of African American history were not uncommon. Woodson's commitment to establishing a distinct category for Black history, separate from a broader American historical narrative, sparked discussions among educators and historians.

Some believed that integrating African American history into a more comprehensive understanding of American history would foster unity, while others, including Woodson, argued that a separate focus was necessary to rectify historical neglect.

Woodson's departure from the NAACP marked a significant episode in his career. This decision was rooted in differences of opinion with NAACP leadership, notably Archibald Grimké. Disagreements centered on Woodson's proposals for the organization to establish an office as a center for Black community concerns and to divert patronage from racially discriminatory businesses. Woodson's departure illustrated his commitment to bold, direct action and his frustration with what he perceived as a more conservative approach within the NAACP.

Views on the role of Christian churches were another point of contention in Woodson's work. In his critique, expressed in "The Mis-Education of the Negro" in 1933, he highlighted limitations within ritualistic churches, arguing that they offered limited opportunities and often required segregation.

Woodson's criticism underscored his belief that such institutions did not effectively reach the masses and contributed to racial inequality rather than serving as catalysts for racial development.

Chapter Seven

Later Years and Death

In his later years, Carter G. Woodson remained steadfast in his commitment to historical research, dedicating himself to preserving and promoting the history of African Americans.

His passion for uncovering neglected aspects of Black history led him to amass a personal collection of artifacts and publications, which served as a testament to his lifelong pursuit of knowledge and understanding. Woodson's collection reflected his belief in the importance of preserving and documenting the diverse experiences and contributions of African Americans throughout history.

One of Woodson's most influential works during this period was "The Mis-Education of the Negro," published in 1933. This seminal work critiqued the educational system's failure to adequately address the needs and aspirations of African Americans, arguing that it perpetuated a cycle of miseducation and disempowerment.

Woodson's insights into the systemic barriers facing Black communities continue to resonate with scholars and activists, underscoring the ongoing relevance of his analysis.

Throughout his later years, Woodson's influence on later generations of scholars, educators, and activists remained profound. His advocacy for the inclusion of African American history in academic curricula and public discourse laid the groundwork for future efforts to promote racial equity and social justice. Woodson's visionary leadership and unwavering dedication to advancing the cause of Black history inspired countless individuals to continue his legacy of scholarship and advocacy.

Tragically, Carter G. Woodson's life was cut short when he passed away from a heart attack on April 3, 1950. His death marked the end of an era but left behind a lasting legacy of intellectual curiosity, resilience, and leadership.

Woodson was laid to rest at Lincoln Memorial Cemetery in Suitland, Maryland, a final resting place befitting his stature as a pioneering figure in African American history. Though he may have departed from this world, Woodson's contributions to the study and celebration of Black history endure as a beacon of hope and inspiration for generations to come.

Chapter Eight

Legacy

Carter G. Woodson's legacy extends far beyond his lifetime, leaving an indelible mark on the study and celebration of African American history. One of his most enduring legacies is the establishment of Negro History Week, which later evolved into Black History Month.

This annual observance continues to serve as a vital platform for recognizing and commemorating the rich heritage and achievements of African Americans. Through educational initiatives, public events, and cultural celebrations, Negro

History Week/Black History Month promotes greater awareness and appreciation of the contributions made by Black individuals and communities throughout history.

Woodson's contributions have been honored through numerous awards, institutions, and landmarks named in his honor. From the Carter G. Woodson Memorial Park in Washington, D.C., to the Carter G. Woodson Institute for African-American and African Studies at the University of Virginia, his name graces institutions that champion the study and preservation of African American history.

Additionally, awards such as the Carter G. Woodson Book Award recognize outstanding contributions to the field of African American studies, ensuring that

Woodson's legacy continues to inspire future generations of scholars and activists.

A cherished ambition of Woodson's was the completion of the Encyclopedia Africana, a comprehensive reference work intended to document the history and culture of people of African descent worldwide. While Woodson did not live to see this ambition realized, his vision continues to inspire efforts to document and preserve the diverse heritage of African peoples.

The Encyclopedia Africana serves as a testament to Woodson's commitment to advancing the study of African American history and ensuring that the contributions of Black individuals are recognized and celebrated on a global scale.

Overall, Carter G. Woodson's legacy is one of scholarship, and advocacy. His pioneering efforts to promote the study of African American history have had a profound and lasting impact, shaping the way we understand and appreciate the rich tapestry of Black experiences.

As we continue to honor his memory and celebrate his achievements, we are reminded of the enduring importance of recognizing and preserving the history and heritage of African Americans for generations to come.

Printed by Amazon Italia Logistica S.r.l.
Torrazza Piemonte (TO), Italy

58506994R10030